Miss Bea's Playtime

Louisa Harding

ROWAN

Hello Miss Bea
Are you going to the playground?

Alice and Bear are already there
swing high, swing low

Miss Bea swings higher and higher
Bear wants a big push

'watch me' says Joe
Whoosh down the slide he goes

'wait for me' cries Miss Bea
as Bear goes 'wheee' down the slide

'wait for me' sweater instructions page 36

'Look out' Joe shouts
'can you catch the ball ?'

'This is fun' Owen laughs
backwards and forwards he swings

Look at Miss Bea jumping
Up and down on the wobbly bridge

'Look at us' Alice holds Bear tightly
as they run across the bridge

Playtime has been lots of fun
It's time to go now, 'bye bye'

The Knitting Patterns
Infomation Page

Introduction
The knitwear in 'Miss Bea's Playtime' has been designed with beginner knitters in mind. The garment shapes are simple to knit and all can be knitted in one colour.
Inspired to pick up your knitting needles we hope you find the instructions easy to understand and the guide to Knitting Techniques a helpful resource to follow.

The knitting patterns
Each pattern has a chart and simple written instructions that have been colour coded making the different sizes easier to identify. E.g. if you are knitting age 2–3 years follow the instructions in red where you are given a choice.

The patterns are laid out as follows:

Age/Size Diagrams
The ages given and the corresponding diagrams are a guide only. The measurements for each knitted piece are shown in a size diagram at the start of every pattern. As all children vary make sure you choose the right garment size, do this by measuring an item of your child's clothing you like the fit of. Choose the instruction size accordingly. If still unsure, knit a larger size, as children always grow.

Yarn
This indicates the amount of yarn needed to complete the design.
If the garment is striped or colour blocked you will have an amount for each colour used.

Needles
Listed are the suggested knitting needles used to make the garment. The smaller needles are usually used for edgings or ribs, the larger needles for the main body fabric.

Buttons/Zips
This indicates the number of buttons or length of zip needed to fasten the finished garment.

Tension
Tension is the single most important factor when you begin knitting. The fabric tension is written for example as 20 sts x 28 rows to 10cm measured over stocking stitch using 4 mm (US 6) needles. Each pattern is worked out mathematically, if the correct tension is not achieved the garment pieces will not measure the size stated in the diagram.
Before embarking on knitting your garment we recommend you check your tension as follows: Using the needle size given cast on 5 –10 more stitches than stated in the tension, and work 5 –10 more rows. When you have knitted your tension square lay it on a flat surface, place a rule or tape measure horizontally, count the number of stitches equal to the distance of 10cm. Place the measure vertically and count the number of rows, these should equal the tension given in the pattern. If you have too many stitches to 10cm, try again using a thicker needle, if you have too few stitches to 10cm use a finer needle.
Note: Check your tension regularly as you knit, once you become relaxed and confident with your knitting, your tension can change.

Back
This is the start of your pattern. Following the colour code for your chosen size, you will be instructed how many stitches to cast on and to work from chart and written instructions as follows:

Knitting from charts
Each square on a chart represents one stitch; each line of squares indicates a row of knitting. When working from the chart, read odd numbered rows (right side of fabric) from right to left and even numbered rows (wrong side of fabric) from left to right.
Each separate colour used is given a letter and on some charts a corresponding symbol. The different stitches used are also represented by a symbol, e.g. knit and purl, a key to the symbols is with each chart.

Knitting with colour
To add some simple variation we have photographed a number of striped and colour blocked designs. The written instructions and chart will inform you when you need to change colour by indicating a new letter or symbol. All the patterns in the book can be knitted using one colour by ignoring the colour change instructions.

Front (Fronts) and Sleeves
The pattern continues with instructions to make these garment pieces.

Pressing
Once you have finished knitting and before you begin to complete the garment it is important that all pieces are pressed, see page 48 for more details.

Neckband (front bands)
This instruction tells you how to work any finishing off needed to complete your garment, such as knitting a neckband on a sweater or edgings on a cardigan.
Once you have completed all the knitting you can begin to make up your garment, see page 48 for making up instructions.

Abbreviations
In the pattern you will find some of the most common words used have been abbreviated, these are listed below:

K	knit
P	purl
st(s)	stitches
inc	increase(e)(ing)
dec	decrease(e)(ing)
st st	stocking stitch (right side row knit, wrong side row purl)
garter st	garter stitch (knit every row)
beg	begin(ning)
foll	follow(ing)
rem	remain(ing)
rev	reverse(ing)
rep	repeat
alt	alternate
cont	continue
patt	pattern
tog	together
cm	centimetres
in(s)	inch(es)
RS	right side
WS	wrong side
K2tog	knit two sts together to make one stitch
tbl	through back of loop
yo	yarn over, bring yarn over needle before working next st to create an extra loop

Knitting Techniques
A simple learn to knit guide

Introduction

Using illustrations and simple written instructions we have put together a beginners guide to knitting. With a basic knowledge of the simplest stitches you can create your own unique handknitted garments.

When you begin to knit you feel very clumsy, all fingers and thumbs. This stage passes as confidence and experience grows. Many people are put off hand knitting thinking that they are not using the correct techniques of holding needles, yarn or working of stitches, all knitters develop their own style, so please persevere.

Casting On –
This is the term used for making a row of stitches; the foundation row for each piece of knitting.
Make a slip knot. Slip this onto a needle. This is the basis of the two casting on techniques as shown below.

Thumb Cast On –
This method uses only one needle and gives a neat, but elastic edge. Make a slip knot 1 metre from the cut end of the yarn, you use this length to cast on the stitches. For a knitted piece, the length between cut end and slip knot can be difficult to judge, allow approx 3 times the width measurement.

1. Make a slip knot approx 1 metre from the end of the yarn, with ball of yarn to your right.

2. Hold needle in RH. With the cut end of yarn held in LH, wrap yarn around your thumb from left to right anti-clockwise to front.

3. Insert RH needle into yarn around thumb, take yarn attached to ball around the back of RH needle to front.

4. Draw through needle to make a loop.

5. Pull on both ends of yarn gently. Creating a stitch on right hand needle.

6. Repeat from 2. until the required number of stitches has been cast on.

Cable Cast On –
This method uses two needles; it gives a firm neat finish. It is important that you achieve an even cast on, this may require practice.

1. With slip knot on LH needle, insert RH needle. Take yarn behind RH needle; bring yarn forward between needles.

2. Draw the RH needle back through the slip knot, making a loop on RH needle with yarn.

3. Slip this loop onto left hand needle; taking care not to pull the loop too tight.

4. Insert the RH needle between the two loops on LH needle. Take yarn behind RH needle; bring forward, between needles.

5. Draw through the RH needle making a loop as before. Slip this stitch onto LH needle.

6. Repeat from 4. until the required number of stitches has been cast on.

How to Knit -
The knit stitch is the simplest to learn. By knitting every row you create garter stitch and the simplest of all knitted fabrics. Garter stitch is reversible and does not curl, it is often used for edgings and bands.

1. Hold the needle with the cast-on stitches in LH. Insert RH needle into first stitch.

2. Take yarn around the back of RH needle, bring yarn forward between needles.

3. Draw the RH needle through the stitch. Drop loop on LH needle

4. Making a loop on RH needle with yarn. One stitch made.

5. Repeat to the end of the row.

How to Purl -
The purl stitch is a little more complicated to master. Using a combination of knit and purl stitches together forms the bases of most knitted fabrics. The most common fabric knitted is stocking stitch, this is created when you knit 1 row, then purl 1 row.

1. Hold the needle with stitches on in LH and with yarn at the front of work, insert RH needle into front of stitch.

2. Take yarn around the back of RH needle, bring yarn to front.

3. Draw the needle through from front to back, making a loop on RH needle.

4. Slip the stitch onto right hand needle. Drop loop on LH needle.

5. Repeat to the end of the row.

Knit 2, Purl 2 Rib -
This uses a combination of knit and purl stitches worked on the same row of knitting to create an elastic fabric. Cast on an even number of stitches (a multiple of 4). With cast on stitches in left hand work as follows: **Row 1**: knit 2 stitches, purl 2 stitches, repeat this action to the end of the row, ending with purl 2 stitches. **Row 2:** Knit 2 stitches, Purl 2 stitches. To create the rib, always knit stitches that were purled on the previous row and vice versa. You can vary ribs by working different combinations of stitches, e.g. knit 1, purl 1 rib, this creates a tight rib or knit 4, purl 4 rib which creates a looser fabric.

Joining in a new yarn -
A new ball of yarn can be joined in on either a right side or a wrong side row, but to give a neat finish it is important you do this at the start of a row. Simply drop the old yarn, start knitting with the new ball, then after a few stitches tie the two ends together in a temporary knot. These ends are then sewn into the knitting at the making up stage, see page 48. Stripes are the simplest way of creating interest and variety to a garment. Join in the new colour as you would join in a new yarn and make the stripes as narrow or wide as you like.

Decreasing One Stitch (K2tog) –
This is the method used to reduce the number of stitches in a row. Worked at the edge to shape a neck or with a yo (yarn over) to create buttonholes. This method can be worked on both knit and purl side of fabric.

1. Hold the needle with the stitches on in LH, insert RH needle into first two stitches.

2. Take yarn around back of RH needle, bring yarn forward between needles.

3. Draw the RH needle through both stitches.

4. Making a loop on RH needle. One stitch made by knitting two stitches together.

Increasing One Stitch –
This method of increasing stitches is used to shape side edges, it can be worked at the end of either a knit or purl row.

1. Hold the needle with the stitches on in LH, insert RH needle into first stitch.

2. Take yarn around back of RH needle, bring yarn forward between needles.

3. Draw through RH needle making loop, one stitch made. Do not drop stitch off LH needle.

4. Reinsert RH needle into the back of same stitch.

5. Take yarn around back of RH needle, bring yarn forward between needles.

6. Draw through RH needle making loop. Two stitches made by knitting into front and back of one stitch.

Casting Off –
This is the method of securing stitches at the top of your knitted fabric. It is important that the cast off edge should by elastic like the rest of the fabric; if you find that your cast off is too tight, try using a larger needle. You can cast off knitwise (as illustrated), purlwise, or in a combination of stitches, such as rib.

1. Hold the needle with the stitches on in LH, knit the first stitch.

2. Knit the next stitch from LH needle, two stitches on RH needle.

3. Using the point of LH needle; insert into first stitch on RH needle.

4. Take the first stitch over the second stitch.

5. One stitch on right hand needle.

6. Rep from 2. until one stitch on RH needle. Cut yarn, draw cut end through last stitch to secure.

Hello Zip Jacket

Age / Size

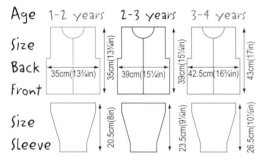

Age	1-2 years	2-3 years	3-4 years
Size Back Front	35cm(13¾in)	39cm(15¼in)	42.5cm(16¾in)
	35cm(13¾in)	39cm(15¼in)	43cm(17in)
Size Sleeve	20.5cm(8in)	23.5cm(9¼in)	26.5cm(10½in)

Yarn

Rowan All Seasons Cotton x 50g balls

A. Sky	2	2	3
B. Tomato	2	2	3
C. Raspberry	2	2	2
Single colour	5	5	6

Needles

1 pair 4mm (US 6) needles for ribs
1 pair 5mm (US 8) needles for main body

Zip

Open-ended zip to fit

Tension

17 sts and 24 rows to 10cm measured over stocking stitch using 5mm (US 8) needles

Back

Using 4mm (US 6) needles and yarn A cast on 60,66,72 sts and work from chart and written instructions as folls:
Chart row 1: K0,0,1 P1,0,2, (K2, P2)14,16,17 times, K2,2,1, P1,0,0.
Chart row 2: K1,0,0, P2,2,1, (K2, P2)14,16,17 times, K1,0,2, P0,0,1.
Cont in rib until chart row 10 completed.

Change to 5mm (US 8) needles, joining in and breaking off yarns as required work in striped st st as folls:
Chart row 11: Knit.
Chart row 12: Purl.
Work until chart row 52,60,68 completed.
Shape armhole
Cast off 5 sts at the beg next 2 rows.
(50,56,62 sts)
Work until chart row 86,96,106 completed.
Shape shoulders and back neck
Cast off 4,5,6, sts at the beg next 2 rows.
Chart row 89,99,109: Cast off 4,5,6 sts, knit until 8 sts on RH needle, turn and leave rem sts on a holder.
Chart row 90,100,110: Cast off 3 sts, purl to end.
Cast off rem 5 sts.
Rejoin appropriate yarn and cast off centre 18,20,22 sts, knit to end.
Chart row 90,100,110: Cast off 4,5,6 sts, purl to end. (8 sts)
Chart row 91,101,111: Cast off 3 sts, knit to end.
Cast off rem 5 sts.

Left Front

Using 4mm (US 6) needles and yarn A cast on 30,33,36 sts and work from chart and written instructions as folls:
Note: 3 sts at centre front are knitted in garter st throughout and are **not** shown on chart.
Chart row 1: K0,0,1 P1,0,2, (K2, P2) 6,7,7 times, K5.
Chart row 2: K3, P2, (K2, P2)6,7,7 times, K1,0,2, P0,0,1.
These 2 rows set the sts.
Cont until chart row 10 completed.
Change to 5mm (US 8) needles and joining in and breaking off yarns as required work in striped st st as folls:
Chart row 11: Knit.
Chart row 12: K3, purl to end.
These 2 rows set the sts.
Work until chart row 52,60,68 completed.
Shape armhole
Cast off 5 sts at the beg next row.
(25,28,31 sts)
Work until chart row 79,89,99 completed.
Shape front neck
Chart row 80,90,100: Purl 6,7,8 sts and leave these on a holder, purl to end. (19,21,23 sts)
Work 1 row.
Chart row 82,92,102: Cast off 4 sts, purl to end.
Dec 1 st at neck edge on next 2 rows.
(13,15,17 sts)
Shape shoulder
Cast off 4,5,6, sts at the beg next row and foll alt row.
Work 1 row.
Cast off rem 5 sts.

Right Front

Using 4mm (US 6) needles and yarn A cast on 30,33,36 sts and work from chart and written instructions as folls:
Note: 3 sts at centre front are knitted in garter st throughout and are **not** shown on chart.
Chart row 1: K3, (K2, P2) 6,7,8 times, K2,2,1, P1,0,0.
Chart row 2: K1,0,0, P2,2,1, (K2, P2) 6,7,8 times, K3.
These 2 rows set the sts.
Cont until chart row 10 completed.
Change to 5mm (US 8) needles, joining in and breaking off yarns as required work in striped st st as folls:
Chart row 11: Knit.
Chart row 12: Purl to last 3 sts, K3.
These 2 rows set the sts.
Complete to match left front, foll chart for right front and reversing shaping.

Sleeves (both alike)

Using 4 mm (US 3) needles and yarn A, cast on 30,32,34 sts and work from chart and written instructions as folls:
Chart row 1: K0,1,2, P2, (K2, P2) 7 times, K0,1,2.
Chart row 2: P0,1,2, (K2, P2) 7 times, K2, P0,1,2.
Cont in rib until chart row 10 completed.
Change to 5mm (US 8) needles, joining in and breaking off yarns as required work in striped st st as folls:
Chart row 11: Inc into first st, knit to last st, inc into last st. (32,34,36 sts)
Chart row 12: Purl.
Cont in striped st st from chart, shaping sides by inc as indicated to 48,52,54 sts.
Work without further shaping until chart row 52,58,66 completed.
Cast off.

Press

all pieces as shown in making up instructions, page 48.

Neckband

Join both shoulder seams using backstitch.
With RS facing and using 4 mm (US 6) needles and yarn B knit across 6,7,8 sts on holder at right front neck pick up and knit 12 sts up right front neck shaping, 24,26,28 sts across back neck, and 12 sts down left front neck, knit across 6,7,8 sts on holder.
(60,64,68 sts)
Rib row 1(WS): K3, (P2,K2) 13,14,15 times, P2, K3.
Rib row 2(RS): K3, (K2,P2) 13,14,15 times, K5.
Work these 2 rows 4 times more.
Cast off in rib.
Complete jacket as shown in making up instructions, page 48.

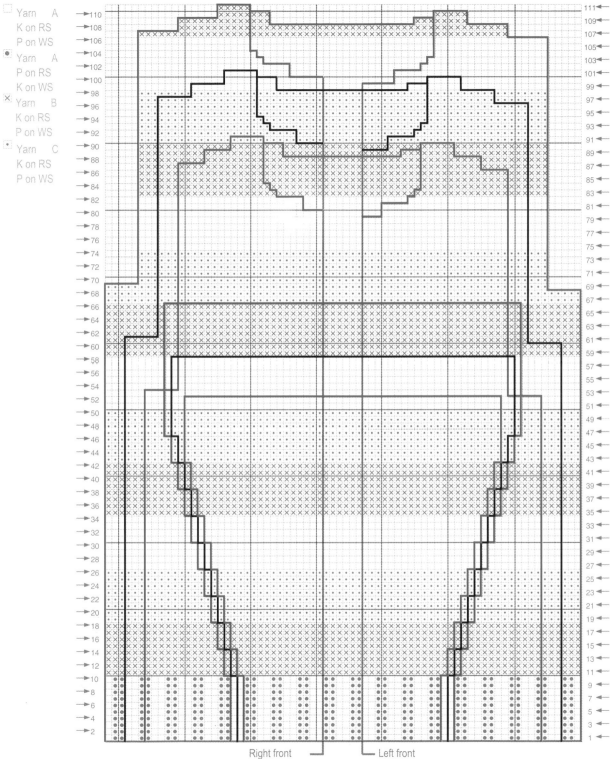

Swing High Cardigan

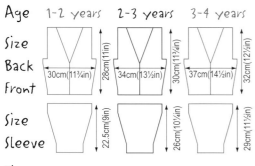

Age	1-2 years	2-3 years	3-4 years
Size Back Front	30cm (11¾in) 28cm (11in)	34cm (13½in) 30cm (11¾in)	37cm (14½in) 32cm (12½in)
Size Sleeve	22.5cm (9in)	26cm (10¼in)	29cm (11½in)

Yarn
Rowan Wool Cotton x 50g balls
Flower   4   4   5

Needles
1 pair 3 ¼ mm (US 3) needles for edging
1 pair 4mm (US 6) needles for main body

Buttons 4

Tension
22 sts and 30 rows to 10cm measured over stocking stitch using 4 mm (US 6) needles

Back
Using 3 ¼ mm (US 3) needles cast on 56,64,72 sts and work from chart and written instructions as folls:
Chart row 1: Knit.
Chart row 2: Knit.
Work these 2 rows once more
Change to 4mm (US 6) needles and cont to work in st st as folls:
Chart row 5: Knit.
Chart row 6: Purl.

Work until chart row 8 completed.
Chart row 9: Inc into first st, knit to last st, inc into last st. (58,66,74 sts)
Chart row 10: Purl.
Cont from chart shaping sides by inc as indicated to 66,74,82 sts.
Work without further shaping until chart row 44,48,52 completed.
Shape armhole
Cast off 6 sts at the beg next 2 rows. (54,62,70 sts)
Work until chart row 84,90,96 completed.
Shape shoulders and back neck
Cast off 4,5,6, sts at the beg next 2 rows.
Chart row 87,93,99: Cast off 4,5,6 sts, knit until 7,8,9 sts on RH needle, turn and leave rem sts on a holder.
Chart row 88,94,100: Cast off 3 sts, purl to end.
Cast off rem 4,5,6 sts.
Rejoin yarn and cast off centre 24,26,28 sts, knit to end. (11,13,15 sts)
Chart row 88,94,100: Cast off 4,5,6 sts, purl to end. (7,8,9 sts)
Chart row 89,95,101: Cast off 3 sts, knit to end.
Cast off rem 4,5,6 sts.

Left Front
Using 3 ¼ mm (US 3) needles cast on 28,32,36 sts and work from chart and written instructions as folls:
Chart row 1: Knit.
Chart row 2: Knit.
Work these 2 rows once more
Change to 4mm (US 6) needles and cont to work in st st as folls:
Chart row 5: Knit.
Chart row 6: Purl.
Work until chart row 8 completed.
Chart row 9: Inc into first st, knit to end. (29,33,37 sts)
Chart row 10: Purl.
Cont from chart, shaping side edge by inc as indicated to 33,37,41 sts.
Work without further shaping until chart row 44,48,52 completed.
Shape armhole and front neck
Cast off 6 sts at the beg next row, knit to last 2 sts, K2tog. (26,30,34 sts)
Cont to dec at neck edge as indicated to 12,15,18 sts.
Work without further shaping until chart row 84,90,96 completed.
Shape shoulder
Cast off 4,5,6, sts at the beg next row and foll alt row.
Work 1 row
Cast off rem 4,5,6 sts.

Right Front
Using 3 ¼ mm (US 3) needles cast on 28,32,36 sts and work from chart and written instructions as folls:
Chart row 1: Knit.
Chart row 2: Knit.
Work these 2 rows once more
Change to 4mm (US 6) needles and cont to work in st st and complete to match left front, foll chart for right front and reversing shaping.

Sleeves (both alike)
Using 3 ¼ mm (US 3) needles and yarn A cast on 38,40,42 sts and work from chart and written instructions as folls:
Chart row 1: Knit.
Chart row 2: Knit.
Work these 2 rows once more.
Change to 4 mm (US 6) needles and cont to work in st st as follows:
Chart row 5: Knit.
Chart row 6: Purl.
Chart row 7: Inc into first st, knit to last st, inc into last st. (40,42,44 sts)
Chart row 8: Purl.
Cont from chart, shaping sides by inc as indicated to 58,62,66 sts.
Work without further shaping until chart row 68,78,88 completed.
Cast off.

Press all pieces as shown in making up instructions, page 48.

Frontband
Join both shoulder seams using backstitch.
With RS of right front facing and using 3 ¼ mm (US 3) needles pick up and knit 33,35,37 sts from cast on edge to start of neck shaping, 37,39,41 sts up right front neck slope to shoulder, 28,30,32 sts across back neck, 37,39,41 sts down left front neck slope, and 33,35,37 sts to end. (168,178,188 sts)
Buttonhole row (WS): Knit 135,145,152 sts, (yo, K2tog, K8,8,9) 3 times, yo, K2tog, K1.
Next row: Knit
Work picot cast off as follows: Cast off 3 sts, *slip st on RH needle back onto LH needle, cast on 2 sts using the cable method, then cast off 5 sts, rep from * to end.
Sew on buttons to correspond with buttonholes.
Complete cardigan as shown in making up instructions, page 48.

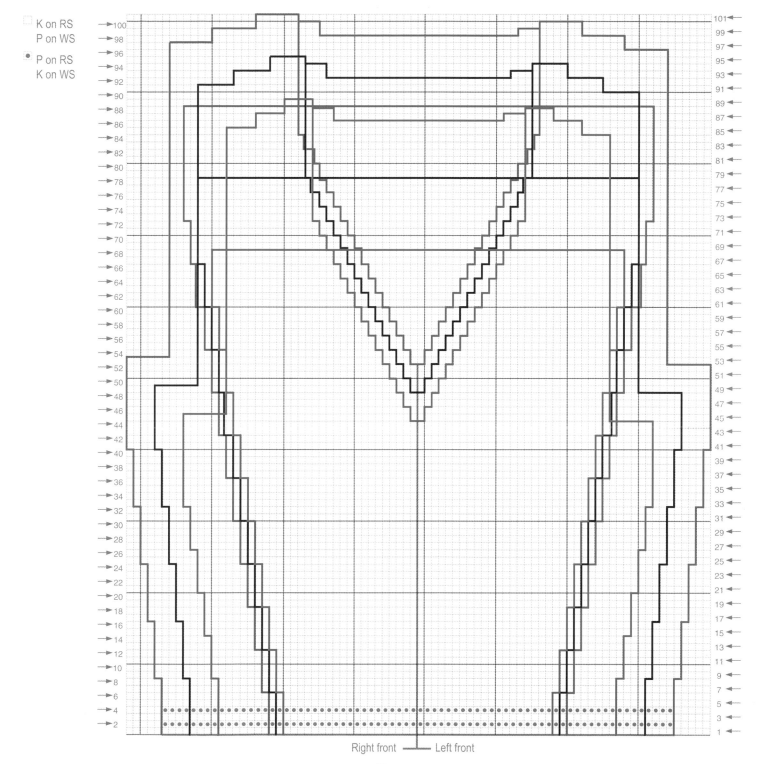

K on RS
P on WS

● P on RS
K on WS

Right front — Left front

31

Big Push Sweater

Age
1-2 years   2-3 years   3-4 years

Size
Back
Front

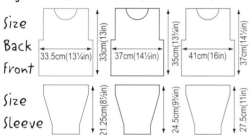

33.5cm(13¼in)   33cm(13in)   37cm(14½in)   35cm(13¾in)   41cm(16in)   37cm(14½in)

Size
Sleeve

21.25cm(8½in)   24.5cm(9¾in)   27.5cm(11in)

Yarn
Rowan All Seasons Cotton x 50g balls

A.Tomato	4	4	5
B.Raspberry	1	1	1
Single Colour	4	5	5

Needles
1 pair 4mm (US 6) needles for edging
1 pair 5mm (US 8) needles for main body

Tension
17 sts and 24 rows to 10cm measured over stocking stitch using 5mm (US 8) needles

Back
Using 4mm (US 6) needles and yarn A cast on 57,63,69 sts and work from chart and written instructions as folls:
Chart row 1: Knit.
Chart row 2: Knit.
Cont in garter st until chart row 10 completed.
Change to 5mm (US 8) needles and joining in and breaking off colours as required work in striped st st as folls:

Chart row 11: Knit.
Chart row 12: Purl.
Work until chart row 52,54,56 completed.
Shape armhole
Cast off 5 sts at the beg next 2 rows. (47,53,59 sts)
Work until chart row 82,86,90 completed.
Shape back neck
Chart row 83,87,91: Knit until 13,15,17 sts on RH needle, turn and leave rem sts on a holder.
Chart row 84,88,92: Cast off 3 sts, purl to end.
Slip rem 10,12,14 sts onto a holder.
Slip centre 21,23,25 sts onto a holder, rejoin yarn to rem sts and knit to end.
(13,15,17 sts)
Chart row 84,88,92: Purl.
Chart row 85,89,93: Cast off 3 sts, knit to end.
Slip rem 10,12,14 sts onto a holder.

Front
Work as for back until chart row 76,80,84 completed.
Shape front neck
Chart row 77,81,85: Knit 16,18,20 sts, turn and leave rem sts on a holder.
Chart row 78,82,86: Cast off 4 sts, purl to end.
Dec 1 st at neck edge on next 2 rows. (10,12,14 sts)
Work without further shaping until chart row 84,88,92 completed.
Slip rem 10,12,14 sts onto a holder.
Slip centre 15,17,19 sts onto a holder, rejoin yarn to rem sts and knit to end.
(16,18,20 sts)
Chart row 78,82,86: Purl.
Chart row 79,83,87: Cast off 4 sts, knit to end.
Dec 1 st at neck edge on next 2 rows. (10,12,14 sts)
Work without further shaping until chart row 85,89,93 completed.
Slip rem 10,12,14 sts onto a holder.

Sleeves (both alike)
Using 4mm (US 6) needles and yarn A cast on 29,31,33 sts and work from chart and written instructions as folls:
Chart row 1: Knit.
Chart row 2: Knit.
Cont in garter st until chart row 10 completed.
Change to 5mm (US 8) needles joining in and breaking off colours as required work in striped st st as folls:
Chart row 11: Inc into first st, knit to last st, inc into last st. (31,33,35 sts)
Chart row 12: Purl.
Cont in st st from chart, shaping sides by inc as indicated to 45,47,51 sts.

Work without further shaping until chart row 56,62,70 completed. Cast off.

Press all pieces as shown in making up instructions, page 48.

Neckband
Join right shoulder seam by knitting sts together on the RS of garment as shown in techniques guide, page 48.
With RS facing and using 4mm (US 6) needles and yarn A and pick up and knit 10 sts down left front neck, knit across 15,17,19 sts on holder, pick up and knit 10 sts to shoulder and 3 sts down right back neck, knit across 21,23,25 sts on holder and pick up and knit 3 sts to shoulder. (62,66,70 sts)
Knit 4 rows ending with a RS row.
Cast off knitwise.
Join left shoulder seam by knitting sts together on the RS of garment as above.
Join neckband seam using backstitch.
Complete sweater as shown in making up instructions, page 48, leaving 10 rows of garter st at bottom edge of garment open for side vent.

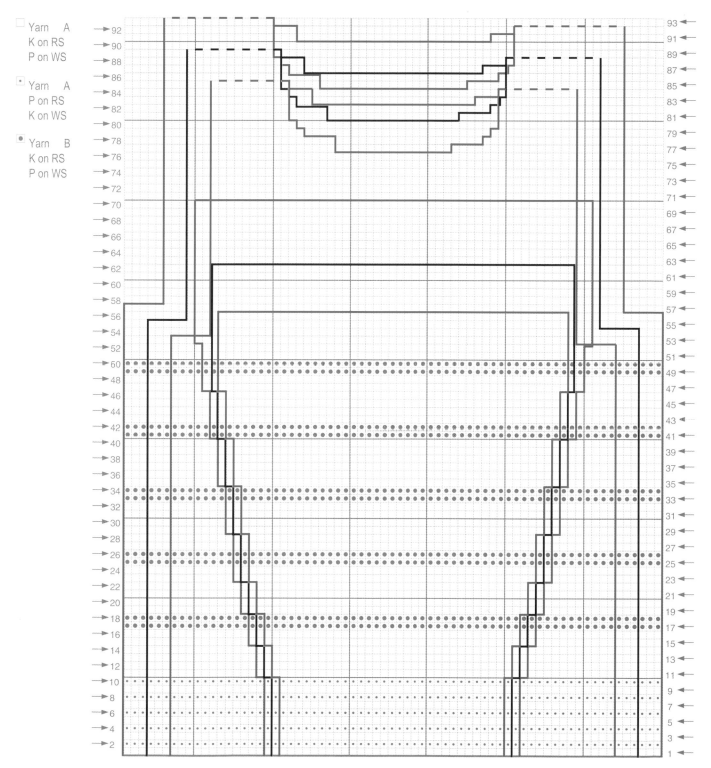

Yarn A
K on RS
P on WS

Yarn A
P on RS
K on WS

Yarn B
K on RS
P on WS

33

Whoosh Zip Jacket

Age

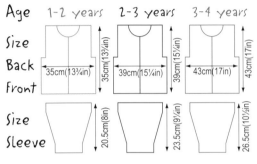

	1-2 years	2-3 years	3-4 years
Size Back Front	35cm(13¾in)	39cm(15¼in)	43cm(17in)
	35cm(13¾in)	39cm(15¼in)	43cm(17in)
Size Sleeve	20.5cm(8in)	23.5cm(9¼in)	26.5cm(10½in)

Yarn

Rowan Handknit Cotton x 50g balls

Blue	8	8	9

Needles

1 pair 3 ¼ mm (US 3) needles for edging
1 pair 4mm (US 6) needles for main body

Zip

Open-ended zip to fit

Tension

20 sts and 28 rows to 10cm measured over stocking stitch using 4 mm (US 6) needles

Back

Using 3 ¼ mm (US 3) needles cast on 70,78,86 sts and work from chart and written instructions as folls:
Chart row 1: Knit.
Chart row 2: Knit.
Cont in garter st until chart row 10 completed.
Change to 4mm (US 6) needles, cont to work in st st as folls:
Chart row 11: Knit.
Chart row 12: Purl.
Work until chart row 62,72,80 completed.
Shape armhole

Cast off 5 sts at the beg next 2 rows. (60,68,76 sts)
Work until chart row 102,114,124 completed.
Shape shoulders and back neck
Cast off 5,6,7, sts at the beg next 2 rows.
Chart row 105,117,127: Cast off 5,6,7 sts, knit until 9,10,11 sts on RH needle, turn and leave rem sts on a holder.
Chart row 106,118,128: Cast off 3 sts, purl to end.
Cast off rem 6,7,8 sts.
Rejoin yarn and cast off centre 22,24,26 sts, knit to end.
Chart row 106,118,128: Cast off 5,6,7 sts, purl to end. (9,10,11 sts)
Chart row 107,119,129: Cast off 3 sts, knit to end.
Cast off rem 6,7,8 sts.

Left Front

Using 3 ¼ mm (US 3) needles cast on 35,39,43 sts and work from chart and written instructions as folls:
Chart row 1: Knit.
Chart row 2: Knit.
Cont in garter st until chart row 10 completed.
Change to 4mm (US 6) needles and work from chart for left front as folls:
Note: 3 sts at centre front are knitted in garter st throughout and are **not** shown on chart.
Row 11: Knit.
Row 12: K3, purl to end.
These 2 rows set the sts.
Work without further shaping until chart row 62,72,80 completed.
Shape armhole
Cast off 5 sts at the beg next row. (30,34,38 sts)
Work without further shaping until chart row 97,109,119 completed.
Shape front neck
Chart row 98,110,120: Purl 8,9,10 sts and leave these on a holder, purl to end. (22,25,28 sts)
Work 1 row.
Chart row 100,112,122: Cast off 4 sts, purl to end.
Dec 1 st at neck edge on next 2 rows. (16,19,22 sts)
Shape shoulder
Cast off 5,6,7, sts at the beg next row and foll alt row.
Work 1 row. Cast off rem 6,7,8 sts.

Right Front

Using 3 ¼ mm (US 3) needles cast on 35,39,43 sts and work from chart and written instructions as folls:
Chart row 1: Knit.
Chart row 2: Knit.
Cont in garter st until chart row 10 completed.
Change to 4mm (US 6) needles and work from chart for right front as folls:
Note: 3 sts at centre front are knitted in garter st

throughout and are **not** shown on chart.
Row 11: Knit.
Row 12: Purl to last 3 sts, K3.
These 2 rows set the sts.
Complete to match left front, foll chart for right front and reversing shaping.

Sleeves (both alike)

Using 3 ¼ mm (US 3) needles cast on 36,38,40 sts and work from chart and written instructions as folls:
Chart row 1: Knit.
Chart row 2: Knit.
Cont in garter st until chart row 10 completed.
Change to 4 mm (US 6) needles, cont to work in st st as folls:
Chart row 11: Inc into first st, knit to last st, inc into last st. (38,40,42 sts)
Chart row 12: Purl.
Cont in st st from chart, shaping sides by inc as indicated to 56,60,64 sts.
Work without further shaping until chart row 62,70,78 completed. Cast off.

Front Pockets (work 2)

Using 4 mm (US 6) needles cast on 24 sts, work in garter st until pocket measures 12cm ending with a RS row. Cast off knitwise.

Sleeve Pocket (work 1)

Using 4 mm (US 6) needles cast on 20 sts, work in garter st until pocket measures 10cm ending with a RS row. Cast off knitwise.

Press

all pieces as shown in making up instructions, page 48.

Neckband

Join both shoulder seams using backstitch.
With RS facing and using 3 ¼ mm (US 3) needles knit across 8,9,10 sts on holder at right front neck, pick up and knit 10 sts up right front neck shaping, pick up and knit 28,30,32 sts across back neck, and 10 sts down left front neck, knit across 8,9,10 sts on holder. (64,68,72 sts)
Work 8 rows in garter st ending with a RS row.
Cast off knitwise.

Making up

Sew pockets to fronts, positioning centrally and 5 cm up from cast on edge.
Sew pocket on sleeve, positioning centrally and 6,7,8 cm up from cast on edge.
Leave garter st edging open at bottom edge of jacket.
Complete as shown in making up instructions, page 48.

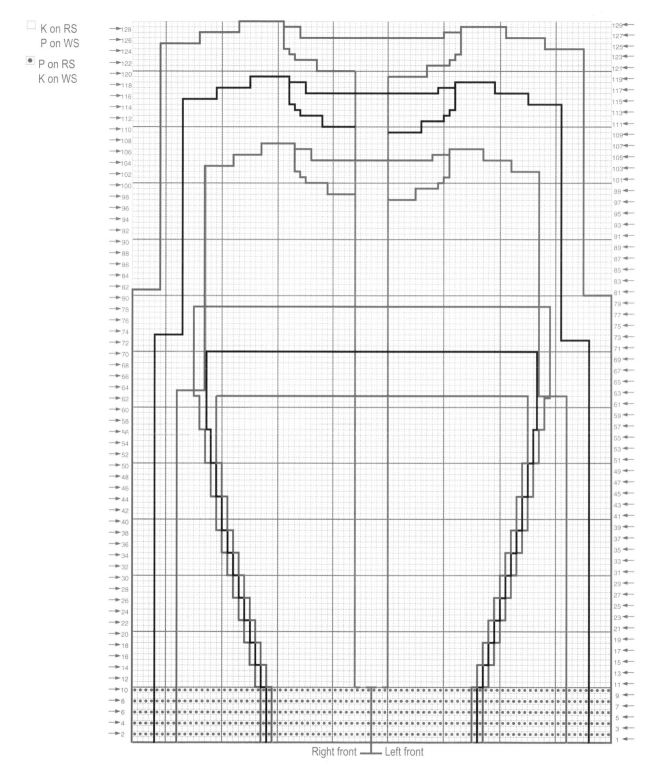

'Wait for Me' Sweater

Age	1-2 years	2-3 years	3-4 years

Size Back Front
33cm(13in) 37cm(14½in) 41cm(16in)
32cm(12½in) 34cm(13½in) 36cm(14½in)

Size Sleeve
21cm(8¼in) 23.5cm(9¼in) 26.5cm(10½in)

Yarn
Rowan Handknit Cotton x 50g balls
Turquoise   5   6   7

Needles
1 pair 3 ¼ mm (US 3) needles for ribs
1 pair 4mm (US 6) needles for main body

Tension
20 sts and 28 rows to 10cm measured over stocking stitch using 4 mm (US 6) needles

Back
Using 3 ¼ mm (US 3) needles, cast on 66,74,82 sts and work from chart and written instructions as folls:
Chart rows 1 & 2: Knit.
Chart row 3: (K2, P2) 16,18,20 times, K2.
Chart row 4: (P2, K2) 16,18,20 times, P2.
Cont in rib until chart row 8 completed.
Change to 4mm (US 6) needles and cont to work in st st as folls:
Chart row 9: Knit.
Chart row 10: Purl.
Work until chart row 56,58,62 completed.

Shape armhole
Cast off 6 sts at the beg next 2 rows. (54,62,70 sts)
Work until chart row 92,98,104 completed.
Shape shoulders and back neck
Cast off 4,5,6, sts at the beg next 2 rows.
Chart row 95,101,107: Cast off 4,5,6 sts, knit until 6,7,8 sts on RH needle, turn and leave rem sts on a holder.
Chart row 96,102,108: Cast off 3 sts, purl to end.
Cast off rem 3,4,5 sts.
Slip centre 26,28,30 sts onto a holder, rejoin yarn to rem sts and knit to end. (10,12,14 sts)
Chart row 96,102,108: Cast off 4,5,6 sts, purl to end. (6,7,8 sts)
Chart row 97,103,109: Cast off 3 sts, knit to end.
Cast off rem 3,4,5 sts.

Front
Work as for back until chart row 88,94,100 completed.
Shape front neck
Chart row 89,95,101: Knit 17,20,23 sts, turn and leave rem sts on a holder.
Chart row 90,96,102: Cast off 4 sts, purl to end.
Dec 1 st at neck edge on next 2 rows. (11,14,17 sts)
Shape Shoulder
Chart row 93,99,105: Cast off 4,5,6 sts at beg next row and foll alt row.
Purl 1 row.
Cast off rem 3,4,5 sts.
Slip centre 20,22,24 sts onto a holder, rejoin yarn to rem sts and knit to end.
(17,20,23 sts)
Purl 1 row
Chart row 91,97,103: Cast off 4 sts, knit to end.
Dec 1 st at neck edge on next 2 rows. (11,14,17 sts)
Shape shoulder
Chart row 94,100,106: Cast off 4,5,6 sts at beg next row and foll alt row.
Knit 1 row.
Cast off rem 3,4,5 sts.

Sleeves (both alike)
Using 3 ¼ mm (US 3) needles cast on 34,36,38 sts and work from chart and written instructions as folls:
Chart rows 1 & 2: Knit.
Chart row 3: P0,1,2 (K2, P2) 8 times, K2, P0,1,2.
Chart row 4: K0,1,2 (P2, K2) 8 times, P2, K0,1,2.
Cont in rib until chart row 8 completed.
Change to 4 mm (US 6) needles and cont to work in st st as folls:
Chart row 9: Inc into first st, knit to last st, inc into last st. (36,38,40 sts)

Chart row 10: Purl.
Cont in st st from chart, shaping sides by inc as indicated to 52,56,60 sts.
Work without further shaping until chart row 60,68,76 completed.
Cast off .

Press all pieces as shown in making up instructions, page 48.

Neckband
Join right shoulder seam using backstitch.
With RS facing and using 3 ¼ mm (US 3) needles pick up and knit 10 sts down left front neck, knit across 20,22,24 sts on holder, pick up and knit 10 sts to shoulder and 3 sts down right back neck, knit across 26,28,30 sts on holder, pick up and knit 3 sts to shoulder. (72,76,80 sts)
Rib row 1 (WS row): K2, P2 to end.
Rib row 2 (RS row): K2, P2 to end.
Work these 2 rows once more.
Knit 2 rows ending with a RS row.
Cast off knitwise.
Complete sweater as shown in making up instructions, page 48.

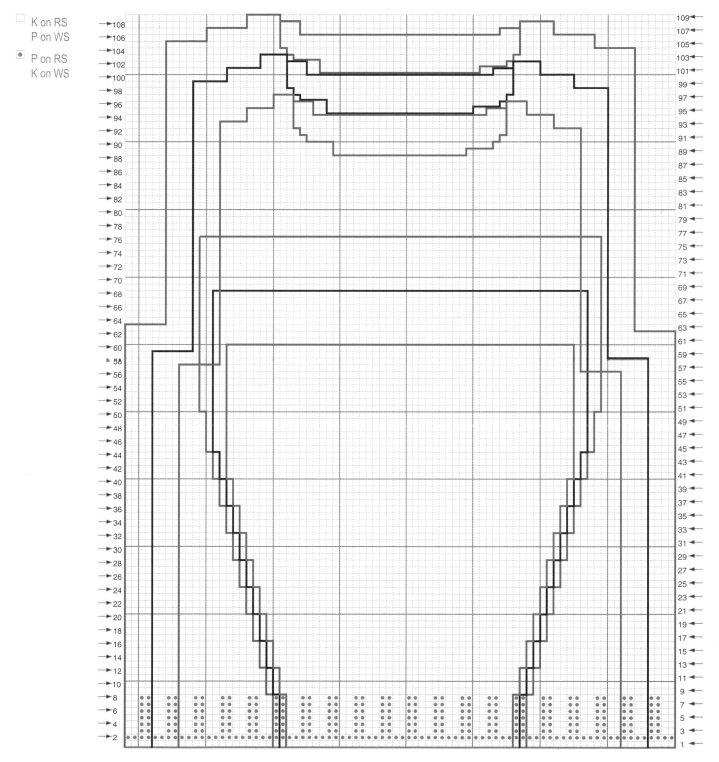

Catch Sweater

Age
1-2 years   2-3 years   3-4 years

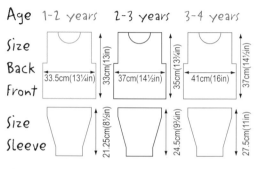

Size
Back
33.5cm(13¼in)   33cm(13in)   37cm(14½in)   35cm(13¾in)   41cm(16in)   37cm(14½in)

Front

Size
Sleeve
21.25cm(8½in)   24.5cm(9¾in)   27.5cm(11in)

Yarn
Rowan All Seasons Cotton x 50g balls

A.Iced Aqua	2	2	3
B.Iced Lime	3	3	3
Single Colour	4	5	5

Needles
1 pair 4mm (US 6) needles for ribs
1 pair 5mm (US 8) needles for main body

Tension
17 sts and 24 rows to 10cm measured over stocking stitch using 5mm (US 8) needles

Back
Using 4mm (US 6) needles and yarn A cast on 57,63,69 sts and work from chart and written instructions as folls:
Chart row 1: P0,3,0 (K3, P3) 9,9,11 times, K3, P0,3,0.
Chart row 2: K0,3,0 (P3, K3) 9,9,11 times, P3, K0,3,0.
Cont in rib until chart row 8 completed.
Change to 5mm (US 8) needles and yarn B cont to work in st st as folls:
Chart row 9: Knit.
Chart row 10: Purl.

Work until chart row 50,52,54 completed.
Shape armhole
Cast off 5 sts at the beg next 2 rows. (47,53,59 sts)
Work until chart row 80,84,88 completed.
Shape back neck
Chart row 81,85,89: Knit until 13,15,17 sts on RH needle, turn and leave rem sts on a holder.
Chart row 82,86,90: Cast off 3 sts, purl to end.
Slip rem 10,12,14 sts onto a holder.
Slip centre 21,23,25 sts onto a holder, rejoin yarn to rem sts, knit to end. (13,15,17 sts)
Chart row 82,86,90: Purl.
Chart row 83,87,91: Cast off 3 sts, knit to end.
Slip rem sts onto a holder.

Front
Work as for back until chart row 74,78,82 completed.
Shape front neck
Chart row 75,79,83: Knit 16,18,20 sts, turn and leave rem sts on a holder.
Chart row 76,80,84: Cast off 4 sts, purl to end.
Dec 1 st at neck edge on next 2 rows. (10,12,14 sts)
Work without further shaping until chart row 82,86,90 completed.
Slip rem sts onto a holder.
Slip centre 15,17,19 sts onto a holder, rejoin yarn to rem sts, knit to end. (16,18,20 sts)
Purl 1 row
Chart row 77,81,85: Cast off 4 sts, knit to end.
Dec 1 st at neck edge on next 2 rows. (10,12,14 sts)
Work without further shaping until chart row 83,87,91 completed.
Slip rem sts onto a holder.

Sleeves (both alike)
Using 4mm (US 6) needles and yarn B cast on 29,31,33 sts and work from chart and written instructions as folls:
Chart row 1: K1,2,3 (P3, K3) 4 times, P3, K1,2,3.
Chart row 2: P1,2,3 (K3, P3) 4 times, K3, P1,2,3.
Cont in rib until chart row 8 completed.
Change to 5mm (US 8) needles and yarn A cont in stocking stitch as follows:
Chart row 11: Inc into first st, knit to last st, inc into last st. (31,33,35 sts)
Chart row 10: Purl.
Cont in st st from chart, shaping sides by inc as indicated to 45,47,51 sts.
Work without further shaping until chart row 54,60,68 completed. Cast off.

Press all pieces as shown in making up instructions, page 48.

Neckband
Using yarn B join right shoulder seam by sts together on the RS of garment as shown in techniques guide, page 48.
With RS facing and using 4mm (US 6) needles and yarn A pick up and knit 9,10,11 sts down left front neck, knit across 15,17,19 sts on holder, pick up and knit 9,10,11 sts to shoulder and 3 sts down right back neck, knit across 21,23,25 sts on holder, pick up and knit 3 sts to shoulder. (60,66,72 sts)
Rib row 1 (WS row): K3, P3.
Rib row 2 (RS row): K3, P3.
Work these 2 rows twice more.
Work rib row 1 once more
Cast off in rib.
Using yarn B join left shoulder seam by knitting sts together on the RS of garment as above.
Join neckband seam using backstitch.
Complete sweater as shown in making up instructions, page 48.

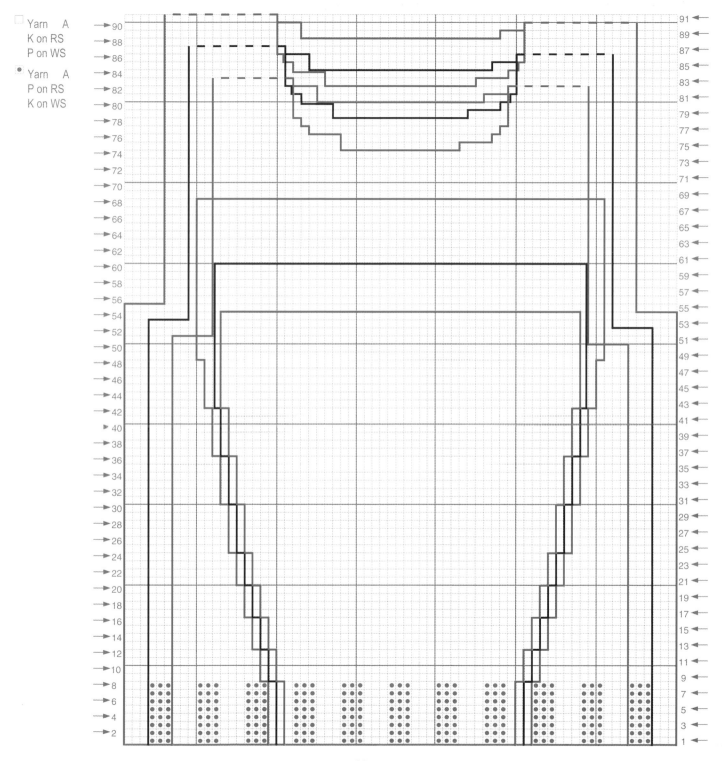

Yarn A
K on RS
P on WS

Yarn A
P on RS
K on WS

39

Tyre Swing Cardigan

Age 1-2 years   2-3 years   3-4 years

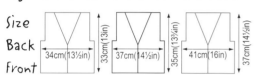

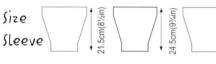

Yarn
Rowan Wool Cotton x 50g balls

A.Aqua	1	1	2
B.Lime	4	4	5
Single Colour	5	5	6

Needles
1 pair 3 ¼ mm (US 3) needles for ribs
1 pair 4mm (US 6) needles for main body

Buttons 5

Tension
22 sts and 30 rows to 10cm measured over stocking stitch using 4 mm (US 6) needles

Back
Using 3 ¼ mm (US 3) needles and yarn A, cast on 74,82,90 sts and work from chart and written instructions as folls:
Chart row 1: K1,0,0, P3,2,0, (K3, P3) 11,13,15 times, K3,2,0, P1,0,0.
Chart row 2: K1,0,0, P3,2,0, (K3, P3) 11,13,15 times, K3,2,0, P1,0,0.

Cont in rib until chart row 10 completed.
Change to 4mm (US 6) needles and yarn B, cont to work in st st as folls:
Chart row 11: Knit.
Chart row 12: Purl.
Work until chart row 62,66,70 completed.
Shape armhole
Cast off 6 sts at the beg next 2 rows. (62,70,78 sts)
Work until chart row 102,108,114 completed.
Shape shoulders and back neck
Cast off 5,6,7, sts at the beg next 2 rows.
Chart row 105,111,117: Cast off 5,6,7 sts, knit until 9,10,11 sts on RH needle, turn and leave rem sts on a holder.
Chart row 106,112,118: Cast off 3 sts, purl to end. Cast off rem 6,7,8 sts.
Rejoin yarn and cast off centre 24,26,28 sts, knit to end. (14,16,18 sts)
Chart row 106,112,118: Cast off 5,6,7 sts, purl to end. (9,10,11 sts)
Chart row 107,113,119: Cast off 3 sts, knit to end. Cast off rem 6,7,8 sts.

Left Front
Using 3 ¼ mm (US 3) needles and yarn A, cast on 37,41,45 sts and work from chart and written instructions as folls:
Chart row 1: K1,0,0, P3,2,0, (K3, P3) 5,6,7 times, K3.
Chart row 2: P3, (K3, P3) 5,6,7 times, K3,2,0, P1,0,0.
Cont in rib until chart row 10 completed.
Change to 4mm (US 6) needles and yarn B, cont to work in st st as follows:
Chart row 11: Knit.
Chart row 12: Purl.
Work until chart row 62,66,70 completed.
Shape armhole
Cast off 6 sts at the beg next row. (31,35,39 sts)
Work until chart row 68,72,76 completed.
Shape front neck
Chart row 69,73,77: Knit to last 2 sts, K2tog.
Chart row 70,74,78: Purl
Cont to dec at neck edge as indicated to 16,19,22 sts.
Work without further shaping until chart row 102,108,114 completed.
Shape shoulder
Cast off 5,6,7, sts at the beg next row and foll alt row.
Work 1 row. Cast off rem 6,7,8 sts.

Right Front
Using 3 ¼ mm (US 3) needles and yarn A, cast on 37,41,45 sts and work from chart and written instructions as folls:

Chart row 1: P3, (K3, P3) 5,6,7 times, K3,2,0, P1,0,0.
Chart row 2: K1,0,0,P3,2,0, (K3, P3) 5,6,7 times, K3
Cont in rib until chart row 10 completed.
Change to 4mm (US 6) needles and yarn B, cont to work in st st and complete to match left front, foll chart for right front and reversing shaping.

Sleeves (both alike)
Using 3 ¼ mm (US 3) needles and yarn A cast on 38,40,42 sts and work from chart and written instructions as folls:
Chart row 1: K1,2,3 (P3, K3) 6 times, P1,2,3.
Chart row 2: K1,2,3 (P3, K3) 6 times, P1,2,3.
Cont in rib until chart row 10 completed.
Change to 4 mm (US 6) needles and yarn B, cont to work in st st as folls:
Chart row 11: Inc into first st, knit to last st, inc into last st. (40,42,44 sts)
Chart row 12: Purl.
Cont from chart shaping sides by inc as indicated to 58,62,66 sts.
Work without further shaping until chart row 66,76,84 completed.
Cast off.

Press all pieces as shown in making up instructions, page 48.

Frontband
Join both shoulder seams using backstitch.
With RS of right front facing and using 3 ¼ mm (US 3) needles and yarn A pick up and knit 53,56,59 sts from cast on edge to start of neck shaping, 33,35,37 sts up right front neck slope to shoulder, 29,31,33 sts across back neck, 33,35,37 sts down left front neck slope, and 53,56,59 sts to cast on edge. (201,213,225 sts)
Rib row 1 (WS row): (K3, P3) 33,35,37 times K3.
Rib row 2 (RS row): (P3, K3) 33,35,37 times, P3.
Work these 2 rows once more.
Buttonhole row (WS): (K1, K2tog, yo, P3, K3, P3) 4 times, K1, K2tog, yo, K3, (P1, yo, P2tog, K3, P3, K3) 4 times, P1, yo, P2tog, K3, (P1, yo, P2tog, K3, P3, K3) 4 times, P1, yo, P2tog, patt to end.
Work 4 more rows in rib.
Cast off in rib.
Sew on buttons to correspond with buttonholes.
Complete cardigan as shown in making up instructions, page 48.

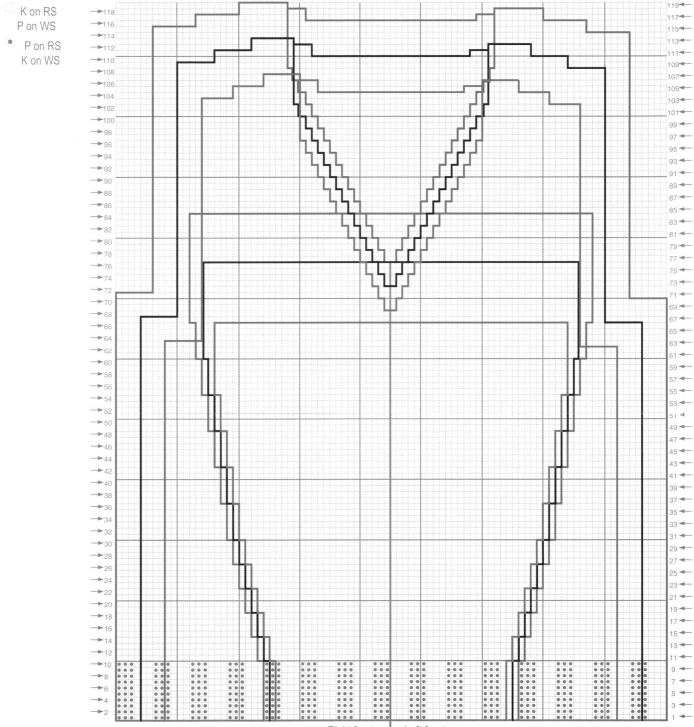

Right front — Left front

41

Jumping Dress

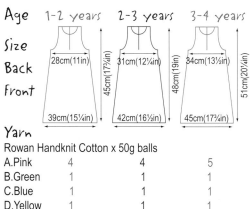

Age 1-2 years 2-3 years 3-4 years

Size

Back

Front

28cm(11in) 31cm(12¼in) 34cm(13½in)
45cm(17¾in) 48cm(19in) 51cm(20¼in)
39cm(15¼in) 42cm(16½in) 45cm(17¾in)

Yarn

Rowan Handknit Cotton x 50g balls

	1-2	2-3	3-4
A.Pink	4	4	5
B.Green	1	1	1
C.Blue	1	1	1
D.Yellow	1	1	1
Single colour	5	5	6

Needles

1 pair 3 ¼ mm (US 3) needles for edging
1 pair 4mm (US 6) needles for main body

Button 1

Tension

20 sts and 28 rows to 10cm measured over stocking stitch using 4 mm (US 6) needles

Back

Using 3 ¼ mm (US 3) needles and yarn A, cast on 78,84,90 sts and work from chart and written instructions as folls:
Chart row 1: Knit.
Chart row 2: Knit.
Rep rows 1 and 2 once more.
Change to 4mm (US 6) needles and joining in and breaking off colours as required work in striped st st as folls:
Chart row 5: Knit.
Chart row 6: Purl.
Work until chart row 8 completed.
Chart row 9: K2tog, knit to last 2 sts, K2tog. (76,82,88 sts)
Chart row 10: Purl.
Keeping striped pattern correct, cont to dec every 8th row as indicated on chart to 56,62,68 sts.
Work without further shaping until chart row 94,100,106 completed.
Shape armhole and divide for back neck
Chart row 95,101,107: Cast off 4 sts at the beg next row, K until there are 24,27,30 sts on RH needle, turn and leave rem sts on a holder.
Work each side of neck separately.
Chart row 96,102,108: Purl.
Chart row 97,103,109: Cast off 3 sts at the beg next row, knit to end. (21,24,27 sts)
Chart row 98,104,110: Purl.
Dec 1 st at armhole edge on next 3 rows and 2 foll alt rows. (16,19,22 sts)
Ages 2-3 years and 3-4 years only
Work 3 rows in st st.
Dec 1 st at armhole edge on next row. (18,21 sts)
All ages
Work without further shaping until chart row 121,129,137 completed.
Shape back neck
Chart row 122,130,138: Cast off 8,9,10 sts, purl to end. (8,9,11 sts)
Dec 1 st at neck edge on next 3 rows. (5,6,8 sts)
Work 1 row.
Cast off rem sts.
Rejoin yarn to rem sts, knit to end. (28,31,34 sts)
Chart row 96,102,108: Cast off 4 sts at the beg next row, purl to end.
Chart row 97,103,109: Knit
Chart row 98,104,110: Cast off 3 sts, purl to end.
Dec 1 st at armhole edge on next 3 rows and 2 foll alt rows. (16,19,22 sts)
Ages 2-3 years and 3-4 years only
Work 3 rows in st st.
Dec 1 st at armhole edge on next row. (18,21 sts)
All ages
Work without further shaping until chart row 122,130,138 completed.
Shape back neck
Chart row 123,131,139: Cast off 8,9,10 sts, knit to end. (8,9,11 sts)
Dec 1 sts at neck edge on next 3 rows.
Cast off rem 5,6,8 sts.

Front

Work as for back until chart row 94,100,106 completed.
Shape armhole
Cast off 4 sts at beginning next 2 rows, and 3 sts at beg foll 2 rows. (42,48,54 sts)
Dec 1 st at each end of next 3 rows and 2 foll alt rows. (32,38,44 sts)
Ages 2-3 years and 3-4 years only
Work 3 rows in st st.
Dec 1 st at each end of next row. (36,42 sts)
All ages
Work without further shaping to chart row 116,124,132 completed.
Shape front neck
Chart row 117,125,133: Knit 11,12,14 sts, turn and leave rem sts on a holder.
Chart row 118,126,134: Cast off 4 sts, purl to end.
Dec 1 st at neck edge on next 2 rows. (5,6,8 sts)
Work without further shaping until chart row 126,134,142 completed.
Cast off rem sts.
Rejoin yarns to rem sts, cast off centre 10,12,14 sts, knit to end.
Purl 1 row
Chart row 119,127,135: Cast off 4 sts, knit to end.
Dec 1 st at neck edge on next 2 rows. (5,6,8 sts)
Work without further shaping until chart row 126,134,142 completed.
Cast off rem sts.

Press all pieces as shown in making up instructions, page 48.

Back neck Opening

With RS facing and using 3 ¼ mm (US 3) needles and yarn A pick up and K20,22,24 sts down right back neck opening and 20,22,24 sts up left back neck opening. (40,44,48 sts)
Cast off knitwise 18,20,22, (K2tog, cast off 1 st) twice, cast off all rem sts.
Join both shoulder seams using backstitch.

Neck edging

With RS facing and using 3 ¼ mm (US 3) needles and yarn A and starting at centre back pick up and knit 13,14,15 sts to shoulder, 10 sts down left front neck, 10,12,14 sts from front neck, 10 sts to shoulder, and 13,14,15 sts to centre back. (56,60,64 sts)

Knit 2 rows.
Cast off knitwise on a WS row.

Armhole edgings (both alike)

With RS facing and using 3 ¼ mm needles and
yarn A with RS of garment facing pick up and
knit 30,32,34 sts from side seam to shoulder
and 30,32,34 sts down to side seam.
(60,64,68 sts)
Knit 2 rows.
Cast off knitwise on a WS row.

Making up

Make a button loop at top opening on right
back, sew button on left side to match.
Sew side seams using back stitch taking care
to match stripes.

☐ Yarn A
K on RS
P on WS

• Yarn A
P on RS
K on WS

○ Yarn B
K on RS
P on WS

☒ Yarn C
K on RS
P on WS

● Yarn D
K on RS
P on WS

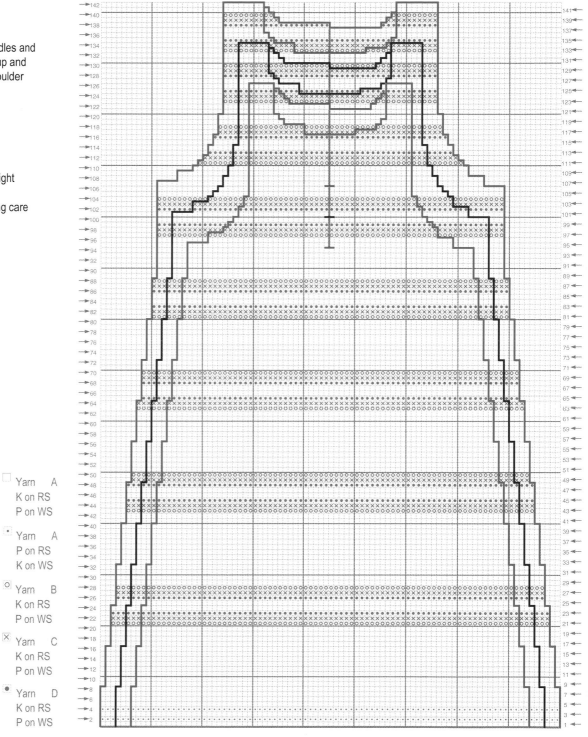

43

Bridge Sweater

Age 1-2 years   2-3 years   3-4 years

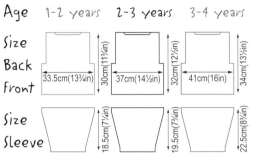

Size
Back
Front

33.5cm(13¾in)   30cm(11¾in)   37cm(14½in)   32cm(12½in)   41cm(16in)   34cm(13½in)

Size
Sleeve

18.5cm(7¼in)   19.5cm(7¾in)   22.5cm(8¾in)

Yarn
Rowan All Seasons Cotton x 50g balls
Iced Aqua   4   5   5

Needles
1 pair 4mm (US 6) needles for edging
1 pair 5mm (US 8) needles for main body

Tension
17 sts and 24 rows to 10cm measured over stocking stitch using 5mm (US 8) needles

Back
Using 4mm (US 6) needles cast on 57,63,69 sts and work from chart and written instructions as folls:
Chart row 1: Knit.
Chart row 2: Knit.
Cont in garter st until chart row 6 completed.
Change to 5mm (US 8) needles cont to work in st st as folls:
Chart row 11: Knit.
Chart row 12: Purl.
Work until chart row 44,46,50 completed.

Shape armhole
Cast off 5 sts at the beg next 2 rows. (47,53,59 sts)
Work until chart row 68,72,78 completed.
Change to 4mm needles work 6 rows in garter st from chart.

Shape back neck
Chart row 75,79,85: Knit until 14,16,18 sts on RH needle, turn and leave rem sts on a holder.
Cast off 3 sts beg next row and foll alt row.
Slip rem 8,10,12 sts onto a holder.
Slip centre 19,21,23 sts onto a holder, rejoin yarn to rem sts and knit to end.
(14,16,18 sts)
Next row: Knit.
Cast off 3 sts beg next row and foll alt row.
Slip rem 8,10,12 sts onto a holder.

Front
Work as for back.

Sleeves (both alike)
Using 4mm (US 6) needles cast on 29,31,33 sts and work from chart and written instructions as folls:
Chart row 1: Knit.
Chart row 2: Knit.
Cont in garter st until chart row 6 completed.
Change to 5mm (US 8) needles, cont to work in st st as folls:
Chart row 11: Inc into first st, knit to last st, inc into last st. (31,33,35 sts)
Chart row 10: Purl.
Cont in st st from chart, shaping sides by inc as indicated to 45,49,51 sts.
Work without further shaping until chart row 48,50,58 completed. Cast off sts.

Press all pieces as shown in making up instructions, page 48.

Neck Edging
Join right shoulder seam by knitting sts together on the WS of garment as shown in the techniques guide, page 48.
With RS facing and using 4mm (US 6) needles pick up and knit 6 sts down left front neck, knit across 19,21,23 sts on holder, pick up and knit 6 sts to shoulder and 6 sts down right back neck, knit across 19,21,23 sts on holder, pick up and knit 6 sts to shoulder.
(62,66,70 sts)
Cast off knitwise WS row.

Join left shoulder seam by knitting sts together on the WS of garment as above. Slip st neck edging neatly together on WS.
Complete sweater as shown in making up instructions, page 48.

□ K on RS
P on WS

• P on RS
K on WS

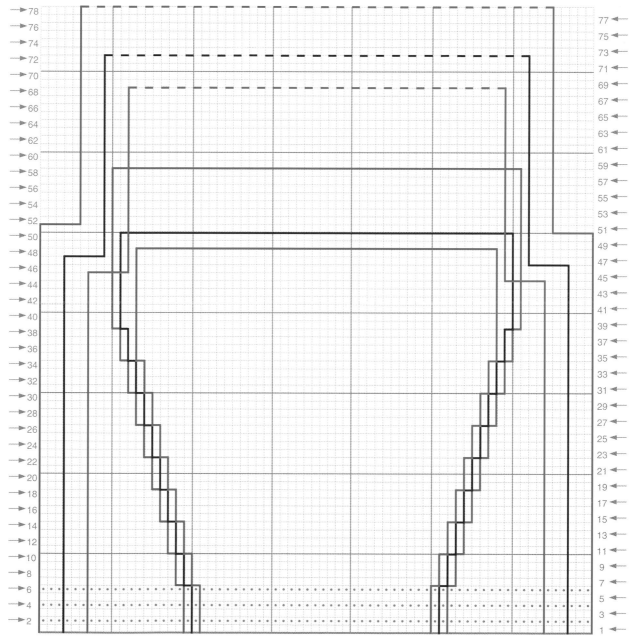

45

Playtime Stripe Sweater

Age	1-2 years	2-3 years	3-4 years

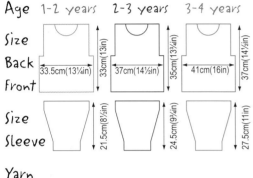

Size Back Front	33.5cm(13¼in) 33cm(13in) 21.5cm(8½in)	37cm(14½in) 35cm(13¾in) 24.5cm(9¾in)	41cm(16in) 37cm(14½in) 27.5cm(11in)
Size Sleeve			

Yarn

Rowan Wool Cotton x 50g balls

A.Aqua	2	2	3
B.Lime	2	2	2
C.Blue	2	2	2
Single Colour	5	5	6

Needles

1 pair 3 ¼ mm (US 3) needles for ribs
1 pair 4mm (US 6) needles for main body

Tension

22 sts and 30 rows to 10cm measured over stocking stitch using 4 mm (US 6) needles

Back

Using 3 ¼ mm (US 3) needles and yarn A, cast on 74,82,90 sts and work from chart and written instructions as folls:
Chart row 1: (K2, P2) 18,20,22 times, K2.
Chart row 2: (P2, K2) 18,20,22 times, P2.
Cont in rib until chart row 10 completed.
Change to 4mm (US 6) needles and joining in and

breaking off yarns as required work in stripe pattern in st st as folls:
Chart row 11: Knit.
Chart row 12: Purl.
Work until chart row 62,66,70 completed.
Shape armhole
Cast off 6 sts at the beg next 2 rows. (62,70,78 sts)
Work until chart row 102,108,114 completed.
Shape shoulders and back neck
Cast off 5,6,7, sts at the beg next 2 rows.
Chart row 105,111,117: Cast off 5,6,7 sts, knit until 7,8,9 sts on RH needle, turn and leave rem sts on a holder.
Chart row 106,112,118: Cast off 3 sts, purl to end.
Cast off rem 4,5,6 sts.
Slip centre 28,30,32 sts onto a holder, rejoin yarn to rem sts and knit to end. (12,14,16 sts)
Chart row 106,112,118: Cast off 5,6,7 sts, purl to end. (7,8,9 sts)
Chart row 107,113,119: Cast off 3 sts, knit to end.
Cast off rem 4,5,6 sts.

Front

Work as for back until chart row 98,104,110 completed.
Shape front neck
Chart row 99,105,111: Knit 20,23,26 sts, turn and leave rem sts on a holder.
Chart row 100,106,112: Cast off 4 sts, purl to end.
Dec 1 st at neck edge on next 2 rows. (14,17,20 sts)
Shape Shoulder
Chart row 103,109,115: Cast off 5,6,7 sts at beg next row and foll alt row.
Purl 1 row.
Cast off rem 4,5,6 sts.
Slip centre 22,24,26 sts onto a holder, rejoin yarn to rem sts and knit to end. (20,23,26 sts)
Purl 1 row
Chart row 101,107,113: Cast off 4 sts, knit to end.
Dec 1 st at neck edge on next 2 rows. (14,17,20 sts)
Shape shoulder
Chart row 104,110,116: Cast off 5,6,7 sts at beg next row and foll alt row.
Knit 1 row.
Cast off rem 4,5,6 sts.

Sleeves (both alike)

Using 3 ¼ mm (US 3) needles and yarn A cast on 38,40,42 sts and work from chart and written instructions as folls:
Chart row 1: K0,1,2 (P2, K2) 9 times, P2, K0,1,2.
Chart row 2: P0,1,2 (K2, P2) 8 times, K2, P0,1,2.

Cont in rib until chart row 10 completed.
Change to 4 mm (US 6) needles and joining in and breaking off yarns as required work in stripe pattern in st st as folls:
Chart row 11: Inc into first st, knit to last st, inc into last st. (40,42,44 sts)
Chart row 12: Purl.
Cont in striped st st from chart shaping sides by inc as indicated on chart to 58,62,66 sts.
Work without further shaping until chart row 66,76,84 completed.
Cast off .

Press all pieces as shown in making up instructions, page 48.

Neckband

Join right shoulder seam using backstitch.
With RS facing and using 3 ¼ mm (US 3) needles and yarn A pick up and knit 10 sts down left front neck, knit across 22,24,26 sts on holder, pick up and knit 10 sts to shoulder and 3 sts down right back neck, knit across 28,30,32 sts on holder, pick up and knit 3 sts to shoulder. (76,80,84 sts)
Rib row 1 (WS row): K2, P2 to end.
Rib row 2 (RS row): K2, P2 to end.
Work these 2 rows four times more.
Cast off in rib.
Complete sweater as shown in making up instructions, page 48.

Yarn A
K on RS
P on WS

Yarn A
P on RS
K on WS

Yarn B
K on RS
P on WS

Yarn C
K on RS
P on WS

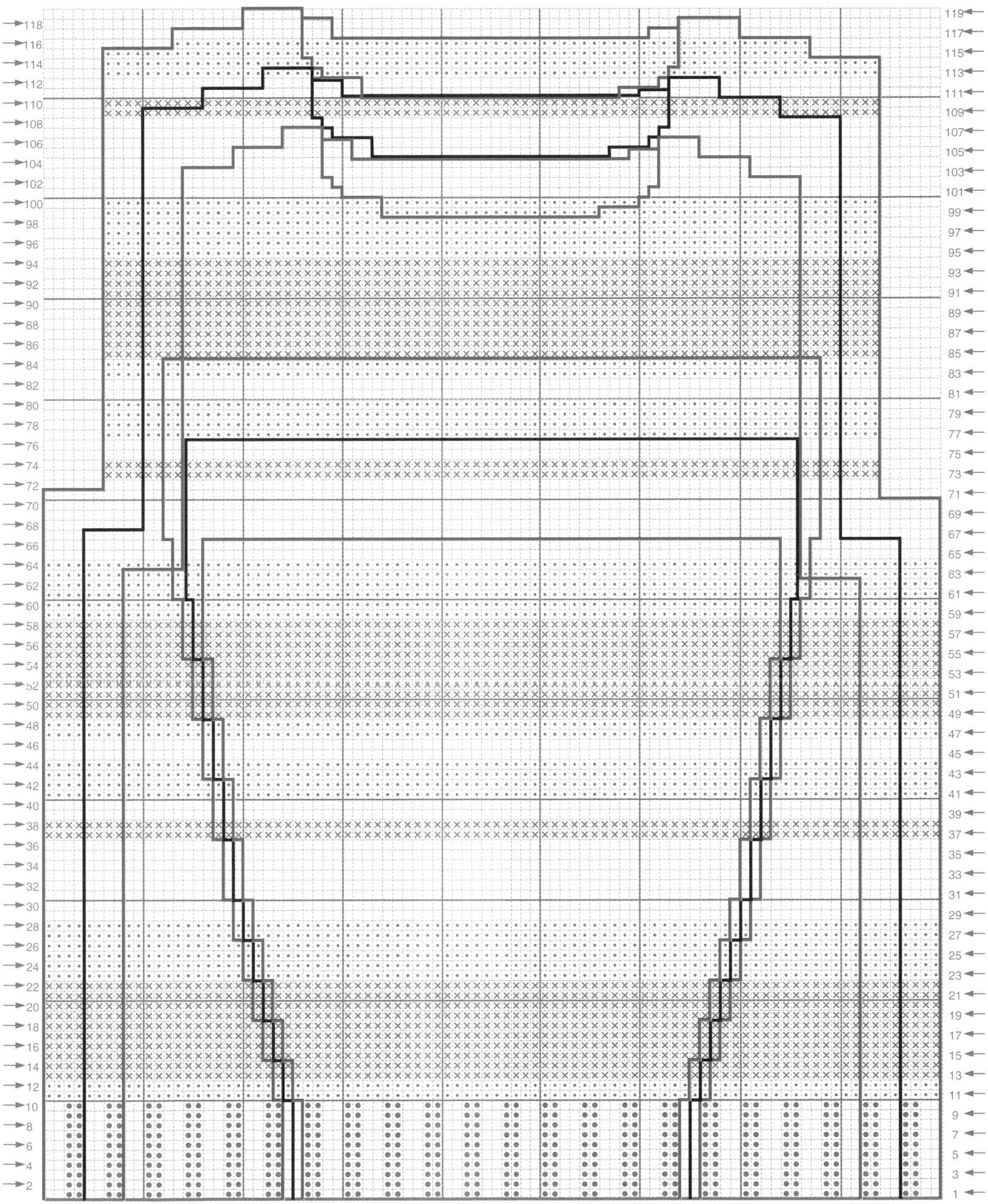

Knitting Techniques
A simple guide to making up and finishing

Putting your garment together
After spending many hours knitting it is essential that you complete your garment correctly. Following the written instructions and illustrations we show you how easy it is to achieve a beautifully finished garment; which will withstand the most boisterous child.

Pressing –
With the wrong side of the fabric facing, pin out each knitted garment piece onto an ironing board using the measurements given in the size diagram. As each yarn is different, refer to the ball band and press pieces according to instructions given. Pressing the knitted fabric will help the pieces maintain their shape and give a smooth finish.

Sewing in ends –
Once you have pressed your finished pieces, sew in all loose ends. Thread a darning needle with yarn, weave needle along approx 5 sts on wrong side of fabric; pull thread through. Weave needle in opposite direction approx 5 sts; pull thread through, cut end of yarn.

Making Up –
If you are making a sweater join the right shoulder seam as instructed in the pattern, now work the neck edging. Join left shoulder seam and neck edging. If you are making a cardigan, join both shoulder seams as in the pattern and work edgings as instructed. Sew on buttons to correspond with buttonholes. Insert square set in sleeves as follows: Sew cast off edge of sleeve top into armhole. Making a neat right angle, sew in the straight sides at top of sleeve to cast off stitches at armhole. Join side and sleeve seams using either mattress stitch or back stitch. It is important to press each of the seams as you make the garment up.

Casting Off shoulder Seams together –
This method secures the front and back shoulder stitches together, it also creates a small ridged seam. It is important that the cast off edge should by elastic like the rest of the fabric; if you find that your cast off is too tight, try using a larger needle. You can cast off with the seam on the right side (as illustrated) or wrong side of garment.

1. Place wrong sides of fabric together. Hold both needles with the stitches on in LH, insert RH needle into first stitch on both LH needles.

2. Draw the RH needle through both stitches.

3. Making one stitch on RH needle.

4. Knit the next stitch from both LH needles, two stitches on RH needle.

5. Using the point of one needle in LH, insert into first stitch on RH needle. Take the first stitch over the second stitch.

6. Repeat from 4. until one stitch left on right hand needle. Cut yarn and draw cut end through stitch to secure.

Picking Up Stitches -

Once you have finished all the garment pieces, pressed them and sewn in all ends, you need to complete the garment by adding a neckband, front bands, or armhole edgings. This is done by picking up stitches along the edge of the knitted piece. The number of stitches to pick up is given in the pattern; these are made using a new yarn. When you pick up horizontally along a row of knitting it is important that you pick up through a whole stitch. When picking up stitches along a row edge, pick up one stitch in from the edge, this gives a neat professional finish.

1. Holding work in LH, with RS of fabric facing, insert RH needle into a whole stitch below the cast off edge, wrap new yarn around needle.

2. Draw the RH needle through fabric; making a loop with new yarn on right hand needle.

3. Repeat this action into the next stitch following the pattern instructions until all stitches have been picked up.

4. Work edging as instructed.

Mattress Stitch -

This method of sewing up is worked on the right side of the fabric and is ideal for matching stripes. Mattress stitch should be worked one stitch in from edge to give the best finish. With RS of work facing, lay the two pieces to be joined edge to edge. Insert needle from WS between edge st and second st. Take yarn to opposite piece, insert needle from front, pass the needle under two rows, bring it back through to the front.

1. Work mattress stitch foundation as above.

2. Return yarn to opposite side working under two rows at a time, repeat..

3. At regular intervals gently pull stitches together.

4. The finished seam is very neat and almost impossible to see.

Back Stitch -

This method of sewing up is ideal for shoulder and armhole seams as it does not allow the fabric to stretch out of shape. Pin the pieces with right sides together. Insert needle into fabric at end, one stitch or row from edge, take the needle round the two edges securing them. Insert needle into fabric just behind where last stitch came out and make a short stitch . Re-insert needle where previous stitch started, bring up needle to make a longer stitch. Re-insert needle where last stitch ended, repeat to end taking care to match any pattern.

Sewing in a Zip -

With right side facing, neatly match row ends and slip stitch fronts of garment together. Pin zip into place, with right side of zip to wrong side of garment, matching centre front of garment to centre of zip. Neatly backstitch into place using a matching coloured thread. Undo slip stitches, zip inserted.

Rowan Overseas Distributors

AUSTRALIA : Australian Country Spinners, 314 Albert Street, Brunswick, Victoria 3056. Tel : (03) 9380 3888

BELGIUM : Pavan, Koningin Astridlaan 78, B9000 Gent. Tel : (32) 9 221 8594

CANADA: Diamond Yarn, 9697 St Laurent, Montreal, Quebec, H3L 2N1. Tel :(514) 388 6188
Diamond Yarn (Toronto), 155 Martin Ross, Unit 3, Toronto, Ontario,M3J 2L9. Tel :(416) 736 6111

DENMARK : Please contact Rowan for stockist details.

FRANCE : Elle Tricot , 8 Rue du Coq, 67000 Strasbourg. Tel : (33) 3 88 23 03 13.

GERMANY : Wolle & Design, Wolfshovener Strasse 76, 52428 Julich-Stetternich. Tel : (49) 2461 54735.
E mail : Wolle_und_Design@t-online.de

HOLLAND : de Afstap, Oude Leliestraat 12, 1015 AW Amsterdam. Tel : (31) 20 6231445.

HONG KONG : East Unity Co Ltd, Unit B2, 7/F, Block B, Kailey Industrial Centre, 12 Fung Yip Street, Chai Wan. Tel : (852) 2869 7110.

ICELAND : Storkurinn, Kjorgardi, Laugavegi 59, Reykjavik. Tel : (354) 551 82 58.

JAPAN : Puppy Co Ltd, TOC Building, 7-22-17 Nishigotanda, Shinagawa-ku, Tokyo. Tel : (81) 3 3494 2395.

KOREA : My Knit Studio, (3F) 121 Kwan Hoon Dong, Chongro-ku, Seoul. Tel : (82) 2 722 0006

NEW ZEALAND : Please contact Rowan for stockist details.

NORWAY : Pa Pinne, Tennisvn 3D, 0777 Oslo. Tel : (47) 909 62 818.
E mail : design@paapinne.no

SWEDEN : Wincent, Norrtulsgaten 65, 11345 Stockholm. Tel : (46) 8 673 70 60.

TAIWAN : Il Lisa International Trading Co Ltd, No 181, Sec 4, Chung Ching N. Road, Taipei, Taiwan R.O.C. Tel : (886) 2 8221 2925.
Chien He Wool Knitting Co, 10 -1 313 Lane, Sec 3, Cmung-Ching North Road, Taipei, Taiwan. Tel : (886) 2 2598 6581

U.S.A.: Rowan USA, 4 Townsend West, Suite 8, Nashua, New Hampshire 03063. Tel : (1 603) 886 5041 / 5043.
E mail : wfibers@aol.com

UNITED KINGDOM : Green Lane Mill, Holmfirth,West Yorkshire, HD9 2DX. Tel : (44) (0) 1484 681881.
Email : mail@knitrowan.com